IT'S A DAD'S LIFE!
CARTOONS BY DAVID SIPRESS

1991

A PLUME BOOK

BOOKS ARE AVAILABLE AT QUANTITY DISCOUNTS WHEN USED
TO PROMOTE PRODUCTS OR SERVICES. FOR INFORMATION PLEASE
WRITE TO PREMIUM MARKETING DIVISION, PENGUIN BOOKS USA INC.,
375 HUDSON STREET, NEW YORK, NEW YORK 10014.

Copyright © 1989 by David Sipress

Some cartoons in this collection appeared previously in the following publications:
Boston Phoenix, Family Circle, Parenting, Lear's, New Woman, Campus Voice.

Library of Congress Cataloging-in-Publication Data

Sipress, David.
It's a dad's life! / cartoons by David Sipress.
p.   cm.
ISBN 0-452-26245-3
1. Fathers—Humor.   2. American wit and humor, Pictorial.
I. Title.
PN6231.F37S57   1989
741.5'973—dc19   88-38339
                                                                    CIP

First Printing, May, 1989

3 4 5 6 7 8 9

PRINTED IN THE UNITED STATES OF AMERICA

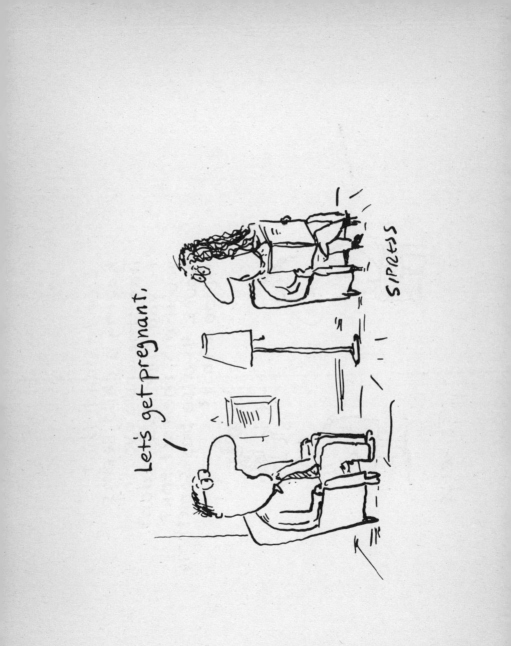

I understand that having a child seems like "the end of youth" to you, Charlie. But don't you think the fact that you're 41 also has something to do with it?
SIPRESS

I'm sick of all these Matthews and Jonahs and Sashas. Let's really go out on a limb and call him Bob.

We're not watching basketball tonight! It's two against one!

SIPRESS

Of course he's sleeping peacefully...
He doesn't have to file a tax return
until 2010.

... and then, of course, after you get the M.B.A., you'll come back and run the business with me.

SIPRESS

SIPRESS

...and then he started crying again and then he spit up all over my sweater, and then I had to change him again and he just kept right on crying, and then...

①

②

Do you think we were right to bring her into a world of rising interest rates and growing budget deficits?

Carol, help! Where's the book that covers this situation??
SIPRESS

Let's see... According to my calculations, if you take care of her for four hours and six minutes, give her one bath, feed her lunch, clean her room, sing her one song, change her twice, read her three stories, and take her to the playground this afternoon, then we'll be completely even for the week.

SIPRESS

Notify all departments, Miss Newman: My son went in the potty last night.

SIPRESS

Now, you two just sit there and be quiet, because you're both been very, very, bad!
SIPRESS

SIPRESS

To tell you the truth, Honey, I don't know what your father does in the bathroom for all those hours. It's one of life's great mysteries.

"Somehow, I don't think the T.V. remote is going to do anything about this, Harry!"

SIPRESS

"It was announced today that Christmas has been cancelled this year to save everybody money."

THE CORRECT CHRISTMAS:

① Caring father and faithful husband.

② Father's satisfied grin as he counts his blessings and reviews his accomplishments.

③ Pipe - Father's ONLY vice.

④ Homey fireplace with stockings and perfect fire.

⑤ Scores of cards from the family's many friends and relatives, business associates, and local tradesmen.

⑥ Perfect wreath.

⑦ Mother's empty chair. She, of course, is in the kitchen, cooking dinner, which will be PERFECT.

⑧ Warm glow.

⑨ Perfect tree and many, many presents, including everything that everyone really wants this year.

⑩ Snow.

⑪ "A Christmas Carol" on T.V. (the original, Alistair Sims version).

⑫ Kindly grandmother.

⑬ Tear of joy.

⑭ Jolly, understanding, wise grandfather, regaling children with stories of the Christmases of his youth when he was very poor.

⑮ Perfect children, who say "no" to drugs, and go to bed as soon as they are told.

sneers

C'mon, Dad! Mom gave Robot Man to me!!

SIPRESS

BOOKS

MAGAZINES

PARENTING
FATHERING
MOTHERING
BROTHERING
SISTERING
AUNTING
UNCLING
First
Cousining

SIPRESS

"Well, Dad, I'll tell you: Every time I face a dilemma about parenting, I ask myself, "What would Dad do?"...And then I do the opposite."

And this is the very spot where Daddy stood during the great "Be-In" of 1967.

SIPRESS

There's my wife, there's my child, there's my toast, there's my coffee... Everything appears to be in order.
SIPRESS

Do as I say, not as I do!!
SOME THINGS DAD GETS TO DO:
- TALK WITH FOOD IN HIS MOUTH...
Blah blah chomp chomp slurp!
- GO IN SWIMMING WITHOUT WAITING ONE FULL HOUR..

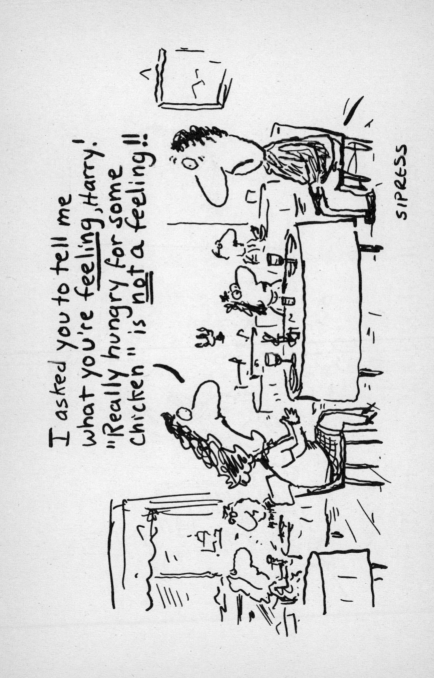

"Wait a second! Hold on a minute! I think this is a scene from _Thirty something_!"

Larry, all I said was let's talk about having another child.

O.K., let's compromise: First we'll talk about baseball and then we'll talk about our relationship!

Someday you'll thank me for this.
26 YEARS LATER:
By the way, Dad, thanks for spanking me that time.
SIPRESS

I remember that... that's plain old running. Not to get to a meeting, not to lose weight, not to catch a train. Just plain old running.
SIPRESS

Gee, Honey, I thought I threw out that tuna casserole ages ago.

Aw, what do you know about life, Dad? You've never even run a computer.
SIPRESS

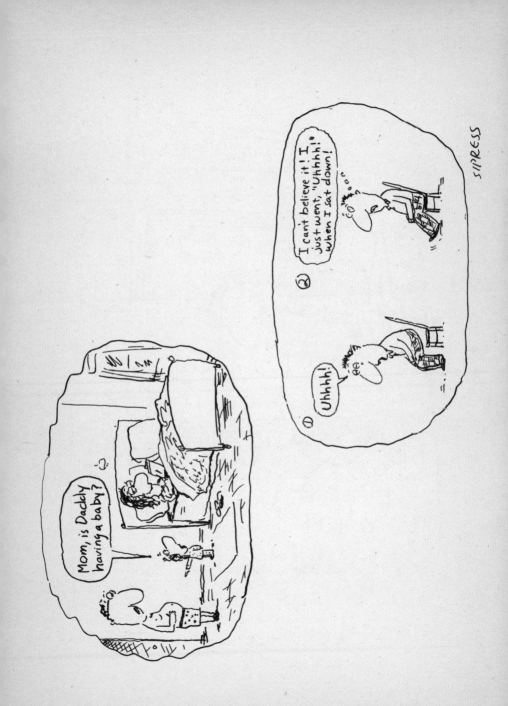

If that leaf lands on the path before I count to three, I'm going to quit the firm, sell the house, move the family back to the city, and write a novel.
SIPRESS

There's an extra fifty bucks in it for you if you take my side today, Doctor.

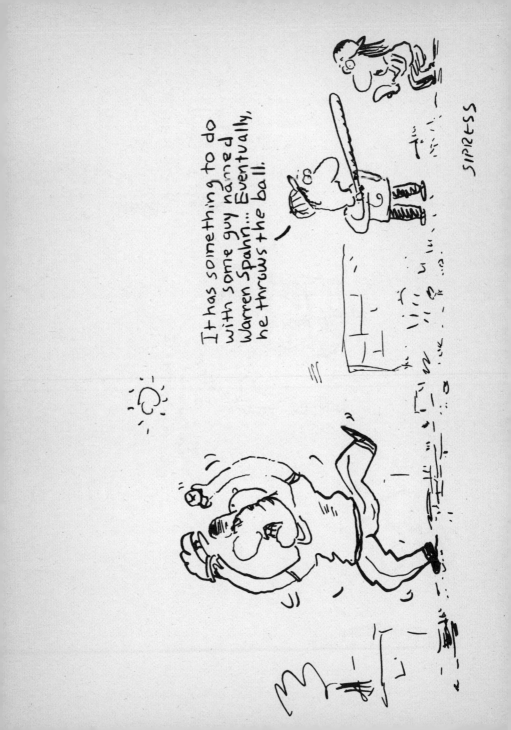

"Frankly, I don't see what the federal cutbacks in education have to do with your "F" in geometry."

SIPRESS

This is money, children. We will fight about it for the rest of our lives.

SIPRESS

Before I decide to
accept this allow-
ance, could you be
a bit more specific
about the "good
boy" stuff?

SIPRESS

Well, son, you're about to be a teenager. That means that in the near future, you'll start to reject every single value, opinion, and point of view that I hold dear. And before you do that, I just want you to know that you have my permission.

SIPRESS

I just wanted to have a little father-daughter talk with you, Honey.

SIPRESS

Well, Fred, your mother seems to think it's time I talked to you about shaving.

SIPRESS

SIPRESS

I asked her to take a walk with me, and she said she had to check her appointment calendar.

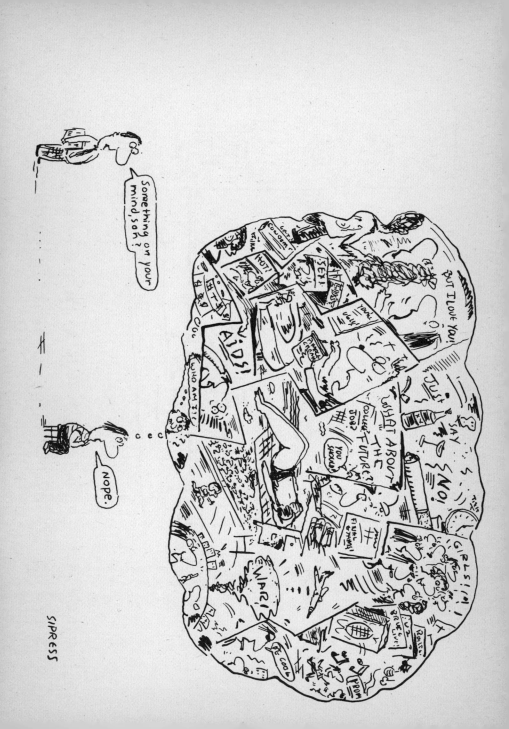

We do appreciate that you're a feminist, Daddy.
But you're also a lousy cook.

No, thanks, Dad. I wouldn't be caught dead in a $7000.00 car.

SIPRESS

SIPRESS

Is that what you're wearing?

You Kids go ahead and have a good time, but please remember, Mike, if my daughter isn't home by one o'clock, I'll have a heart attack, and I really don't think you want to have that on your conscience for the rest of your life.

SIPRESS

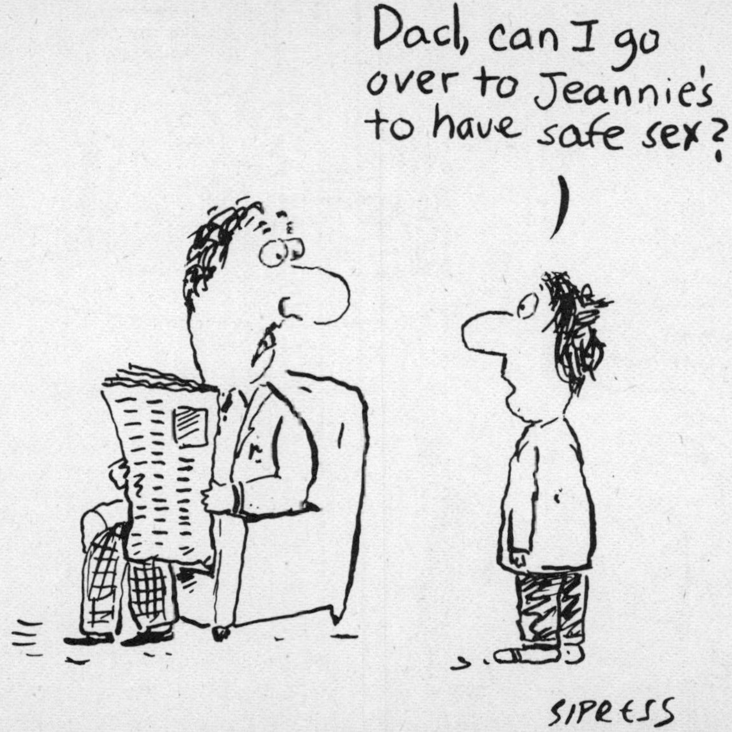
Dad, can I go over to Jeannie's to have safe sex?
SIPRESS

Of course I'm glad he's becoming his own person. I just wish he were becoming someone else.

SIPRESS

Don't you worry, Dear, it's just a phase he's going through.

I just wanted to let you know that after think-ing about it, I totally support your decision to make the biggest mistake of your life and go to art school.

SIPRESS

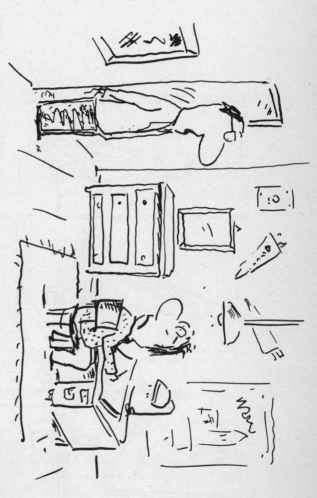

...SIPRESS

Dad, I'd like you to meet Professor Litman. He's my father figure.

I know she's twenty-eight,
I know she's lived with
two different men, and
I know she owns a
diaphragm. But that still
doesn't prove she's not
a virgin!

SIPRESS

Well, I can't tell you how pleased we are
that Sally is finally dating someone
with a decent job.

SIPRESS

SIPRESS

Before I actually go out and look for a job, Dad, I just wanted to check and make absolutely sure there's no chance you would support me for the rest of my life.

The reason I never apologized to you during your childhood is that I never was wrong.

ABOUT THE AUTHOR

David Sipress is the author of the bestselling cartoon collection IT'S A MOM'S LIFE! A cartoonist and sculptor, he presently resides in New York City. His work has appeared in *Spy, Harper's, New Woman, Family Circle, Psychology Today,* and *The Boston Phoenix.*

PLUME TICKLES YOUR FUNNYBONE

☐ **MAXINE!** by Marian Henley. The first cartoon novel featuring the fabulous feminist and flirt, Maxine. Through her disasterous affair with the debonair T.S. Maverick and her tortured and hilarious recovery, Maxine always follows one rule—never, under any circumstances, remove your sunglasses! "Chonicles the inner flights of fancy and frenzy taken by one thoroughly modern woman." —*Utne Reader* (259991—$6.95)

☐ **THE WIT AND WISDOM OF MARK TWAIN** edited by Alex Ayres. An A to Z compendium of quotes from the greatest American humorist-philos-opher. This delightful new anthology has collected the best of Twain, his most trenchant—or most outrageous—quips, sayings, one-liners, and humor— not only from his beloved novels, but from his speeches, letters, and conversations. Arranged alphabetically by topic, from ADAM to YOUTH, here you will delight in sayings as fresh as when Twain first coined them. A wonderul book for browsing . . . or for reading and laughing out loud! (009820—$7.95)

☐ **HOLLENHEAD** by Sabin C. Streeter. From the happily dog-eared pages of the *Yale Daily News* comes this hilarious send-up of the college scene. "In the world of art, precocious talent is a rare commodity. Among the chosen few is Yale's Sabin Streeter, a comic strip creator extraordinaire." —*Interview* (259541—$5.95)

☐ **THE OFFICIAL M.D. HANDBOOK** by Anne Eva Ricks, M.D. Are you M.D. material? Find out with this hilarious handbook of tricks and secrets of the medical trade. Dr. Ricks offers an irreverent and humorous look at the life of a doctor, from med school to malpractice insurance. (254388—$4.95)

☐ **THE UNOFFICIAL NURSE'S HANDBOOK** by Nina Schroeder, R.N., with Richard Mintzer. Find out what makes a nurse tick! Nina Schroeder will have you in stitches as she introduces you to the best and worse moments in a nursing career. From favorite nurse entertainment to famous phrases they teach in nursing school, the contents of this book are guaranteed to split your sides. (258995—$6.95)
